Hydroponics Gardening

A DIY Guide to Growing
Vegetables
(B&W Version)

By

RAINA CAIN

Copyright © Raina C., 2018

Disclaimer

All Rights Reserved. No part of this book may be reproduced or transmitted in any form or by any means, mechanical or electronic, including photocopying or recording, or by any information storage and retrieval system, or transmitted by email without permission in writing from the publisher. This book is for entertainment purposes only. The views expressed are those of the author alone.

Table of Contents

Introduction...	1
Chapter 1: Hydroponic Systems for Growing Plants...........	3
Chapter 2: How to Construct a Hydroponic System...........	10
Chapter 3: Common Problems with Hydroponic Systems.....	15
Chapter 4: Plants Best Suited for a Hydroponic Garden.......	19
Chapter 5: Growing the Most Common Vegetables Hydroponically..	24
Chapter 6: The Preparation and Use of Homemade Fertilizers	41
Chapter 7: Frequently Asked Questions...........................	49
Conclusion...	56
Other Related Books...	58

Introduction

Hydroponic gardening simply means that you grow your plants without actually planting them in soil. Plants need three basic things to be able to grow: light for photosynthesis, nutrients and water. In a traditional garden they absorb the nutrients and moisture through their root systems from the soil they are planted in. In a hydroponics garden they receive their nutrients and moisture directly from the water-based nutrient solution you provide them with. Only the roots need to come into contact with this solution to absorb what they need, therefore there is no need for soil. If your garden is situated indoors, you will have to provide your plants with the necessary light as well. This can easily be done by installing grow lights.

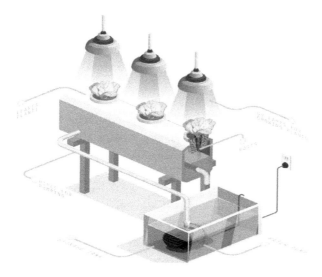

Hydroponics or the method of growing plants in water without soil may sound like something from a science fiction movie. The fact is that it has been in practice since the seventh century BC. But only in the last decade or so has is it really gained a foothold amongst commercial farmers as well as home gardeners.

There are many reasons why hydroponic gardening is becoming more and more popular, both with commercial farmers and individual gardeners. The quality of the produce when grown in a water-based system is of a much higher quality. Plants grown traditionally are subjected to many variables like soil quality, sudden changes in temperatures, pests and diseases etc. In a well-organized hydroponics grow room or greenhouse all these elements can be controlled, even the temperature and humidity. This implies that the gardener or farmer is not dependent on the weather, but can grow plants all year round, making hydroponics a much more profitable enterprise. Plants grown in a water-based nutrient solution also yield more than those grown in soil.

Another benefit is that hydroponic gardens need a lot less space. Whether you chose to grow only one kind of vegetable in a small area inside your spare room at home or on your balcony, you will be able to fulfil your life-long desire to grow your own vegetables. Bigger enterprises are even buying up old buildings in urban areas to turn them into hydroponic gardens combining vertical gardening methods with aquatic-based systems.

Growing vegetables hydroponically inside your home is a lot less messy than the traditional methods. And to top it all, the plants help to clean the air and release oxygen into your home.

So, with a few pieces of equipment, a little effort and the correct information, anyone can now grow their own vegetables or plants at home using a hydroponic system. In this book I will provide you with all the information you need, point out a few pitfalls and answer the most frequently asked questions. After reading this you will see how easy it really is and will surely be inspired to start right away!

Chapter 1

Hydroponic Systems for Growing Plants

The word hydroponics suggests the fact that water forms the basis of the growing medium. Plants are grown in a water-based solution rich in nutrients, without the use of soil. Instead, other inert mediums like Rockwool, vermiculite, peat moss, clay pellets or perlite are used to support the root systems of the plants. The basic assertion is that this system allows the roots of the plants to have direct access to the nutrients and the oxygen in the water-based solution, both of which are the basic necessities for growth.

In this chapter I will discuss the benefits of choosing hydroponics to grow your plants and the different hydroponic systems you can choose from. Maybe you are not planning to switch to a hydroponic system just yet? Nevertheless, you will get ample information about exactly what plants require during their various growing phases, so read on!

Why Select Hydroponic Gardening

Whatever you want to grow; vegetables, fruit or flowers, this system is a first-rate choice. It enables you to carefully control all the variables which can affect the growth of your plants. Plant quality, as well as the amount of produce your plants yield may exceed any system based on soil if you fine-tune your hydroponics system.

Always wanted to grow the yummiest, juiciest fruit or the biggest veggies? Then switch to the hydroponics system. For the first-time water-based gardener it may all sound a little intimidating, but as soon as you get the hang of all the equipment and what to do, it will be as easy as pie. Always start on a small scale, keep things simple and you cannot go wrong.

A Few Pros and Cons

Efficiency

This must easily be the most efficient way of gardening for various reasons. Very little is wasted since you use only what your plants need to prosper. Because the plant roots are in direct contact with water, the waste of moisture is minimized. You will need less fertilizer too, as less will be lost due to drainage. Gone are all your weed problems and issues with pests like insects will occur a lot less often. However, you will have to know your individual plants, and be well informed about all their individual needs.

Cost

A main drawback of a hydroponic gardening system is the cost involved. The initial outlay, as well as running operational costs are usually higher than those for traditional soil gardens. Having said that, I must point out that this is only true if the existing soil in your traditional garden is of a good, high quality. If that is not the case, you will need extensive adjustments with fertilizers and your costs could escalate quite a lot. In this last instance you may even find a hydroponic system less costly.

Space

Hydroponic gardening systems make gardening possible for everyone. You do not need a huge yard and even an apartment dweller can become a hydroponics gardener. The root systems of plants grown in water are a lot smaller and need less space. With the correct use of artificial lights, you can easily grow your plants indoors and crop rotation is no longer a constraint like they are in the case of traditional gardens.

Harvests and Crop Yields

After investing some money to get the equipment for your hydroponic system, you will soon be rewarded for that initial outlay by the surprising high yield you receive from your plants. Even in areas unsuitable for normal gardening like parts of the country with harsh climates or deserts, a hydroponic system provides all the nutrients and moisture necessary for plants to flourish. Neither are you limited by the seasons; your plants will produce their harvests throughout the year. Once you have become experienced, you may even be able to bring about earlier harvests than in normal gardens.

Different Kinds of Hydroponics Systems

There are a number of different systems available for the hydroponics gardener to choose from, even hybrids which combine various systems together into one. The reason for this multitude of varieties is because there are many techniques which can be used to make the water-based nutrients available to the plants. The following are a few which you may consider.

Deepwater Culture

The simplest and easiest method to use is known as DWC or Deepwater Culture. It is also referred to as a reservoir system. This hydroponic method allows for the entire plant root system to be submerged in the nutrient solution. The plant roots are prevented from drowning by the use of a simple aquarium pump which pumps oxygen into the solution and aerates the roots. It is important not to allow light into the system as it will encourage the growth of algae and may cause you endless problems.

The DWS does not use any spray or drip emitters. If you are an organic gardener, this is your best choice since organic nutrients usually are more inclined to clog up.

Nutrient Film Techniques

Plants grown with the NFT do not have their roots submerged in a nutrient solution like the previously discussed system. Instead, a nutrient solution flows over the plant roots in a continuous flow. The flow is managed by tilting the plant container slightly so that gravity can do its trick.

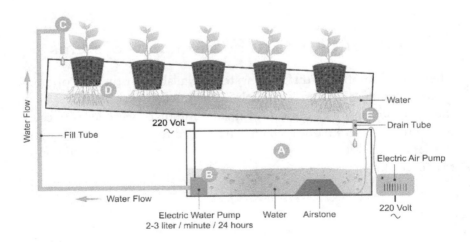

A. Nutrient tank stores nutrient
B. Nutrient water pump circulates nutrient
C. Nutrient flows into grow channel
D. Nutrient absorbed by plant roots
E. Unused nutrient flows back into tank

Because the plant roots are not completely submerged in water and only their tips dip into the solution, they can absorb much more oxygen out of the available air around them – a lot more than they are able to from the solvent they grow in. And we all know that more oxygen means faster and better growth.

Aeroponics

This system uses a mist to spray the plant roots with the necessary nutrients while the roots are suspended and exposed to the air. Two methods can be used to apply the nutrient solution to these dangling roots. Firstly, you can spray them using a fine nozzle. A second method involves the use of a so-called pond fogger. In case your choice falls on the latter, make sure to use a disc which is coated with Teflon to reduce the maintenance load.

If you feel slightly overwhelmed with the idea of constructing your own aeroponics system, you might consider purchasing an AeroGarden, the commercialized version. The set-up requires very little effort and all the supplies and support you need are included in the package.

Wicking

This is by far the most cost effective and simplest hydroponics method. This concept means that you use some kind of material like cotton, and place one end into your nutrient solution while the rest surrounds your choice of growing medium. The wick transfers the nutrients to all the plant roots.

You can simplify this method even further: Simply suspend one end of your wicking material into your nutrient solution while the other end goes into the growth medium you use for your plants. I recommend vermiculite or perlite for your wick. Stay away from peat moss, Rockwool or coconut coir; they tend to absorb higher quantities of the solution and may suffocate your plants.

Ebb and Flow

This system works exactly like its name implies. First it floods the plants' growing space with nutrients after which the solution is allowed to slowly drain away, and flow back into the nutrient reservoir. This is repeated at specifically timed intervals. A timer controls the timing of these intervals to make sure your plants received the correct quantities of nutrients.

This flooding and draining hydroponics system works especially well for plants which are used to dry spells. Certain plants when experiencing a dry period grow their root systems more extensively, searching for adequate moisture. A larger root system means that the plant is able to absorb larger quantities of nutrients and grow faster and bigger.

Drip System

This is a rather simple, straight forward hydroponic system. It administers a slow, steady feed of the nutritious solution to whatever hydroponic medium you choose for your plants. I recommend that you focus on a medium with slow drainage capacity like peat moss, Rockwool or coconut coir. If you prefer a medium which drains faster, make sure you use an emitter that drips faster too.

There is a downside to this system; the emitters or drippers tend to clog. Over time there is a build-up of the small particles of nutrients in the drippers and eventually they will block the tiny holes of the emitters. This is especially the case with organic nutrients.

Useful Tips

- I recommend that you change the nutrient fluid in your reservoir every 2 to 3 weeks.
- The temperature of the water in your reservoir should stay between sixty-five and seventy-five degrees Fahrenheit. Use a water chiller or heater to control the temperature of the reservoir water.
- Increase the circulation of your nutrient fluid to keep it oxygenated by using an air pump connected to one or two air stones by a flexible tube.
- If you notice that your plants do not thrive and become distorted or discolored, the first step is to check the pH, it may need adjusting. If this does not seem to cause the problem, use Clearex or any similar solution to flush your complete system.
- Always make sure you follow the cycle of plant feeding which is provided with the nutrients you purchase.
- After every growing cycle, you should first flush, then clean and lastly sterilize the entire hydroponics system. Make sure to drain the reservoir and clean it from all debris. Once you have done this, run the complete system for a day using a mixture of water and bleach without chlorine. The ratio is an eighth cup of bleach to a gallon of water. Lastly wash out all traces of bleach by flushing the system with water only.

Now that you have a good overview of which hydroponics systems are available and the pros and cons of these systems, I will proceed to discuss them in more detail.

Chapter 2

How to Construct a Hydroponic System

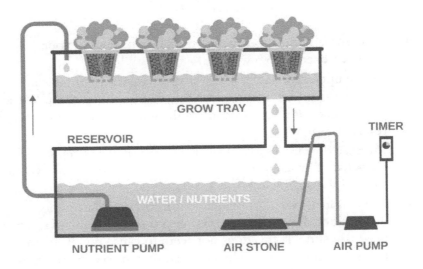

So, you have decided to embark on your career as a gardener with a difference, a hydroponics gardener. Now you have to start on your equipment. There is no need to go out and purchase expensive equipment like grow lights, a reservoir, nutrients or a complete hydroponic system to start a hydroponic garden of your own. For a lot less money you can construct it all yourself and believe me it is not a complicated task once you know how to go about it. With the correct information anyone can do it. You can find inexpensive, commercial nutrients to use; just look around for what is available. And even costly grow lights will not be needed if you have an area with its own natural sunlight. It does not matter which plants you intend to grow; most hydroponic systems consist of only five or six basic elements.

The Basic Parts of a Hydroponic System

Growing Tray/Chamber

This is where your plants are placed, where their roots will receive their nutrients and moisture to enable them to grow. It forms the container for your plants' root systems, and forms the support area for the plants where their roots will come into contact with the nutrient compound. The growing chamber also keeps out pests, and protects your plants against heat and light. The latter is quite important because the plant root area should always be kept light proof and cool. Prolonged light damages the roots and too much heat causes stress to the plants, resulting in flower and fruit drop. Always keep the nutrient compound at the correct temperature too since this has a direct influence on the health of the plants. You want to keep your plants under conditions comfortable to them so that they can thrive.

The shape and size of your growing trays will depend entirely on which plants you want to grow, and also on the kind of system you want to construct. Of course, larger plants with their more extensive root systems will need bigger spaces to accommodate them. You can utilize almost anything to use as a growing chamber; the choices are endless and so are the designs. Just steer away from anything metallic. It may eventually start to corrode and react with your nutrient solution. Look around, even in your own home, for ideas before you go out and buy a growing tray. You may just have the ideal container in your home already.

Reservoir

This is the container which will hold your nutrient compound. This solution is made up of water and the nutrients your plants will need. The way you construct your reservoir will depend entirely on the kind of hydroponics system you plan to build. By installing a timer, the solution may be pumped to the growing tray from the reservoir, or without the use of a pump in a continuous stream. Otherwise the plant roots can hang with their tips or the entire root system in the solution, turning the reservoir into the growing tray.

Reservoirs can be made from any plastic container but it should hold sufficient water and be leak proof. Always clean out the container thoroughly before you use it. It is important for your reservoir container to be light proof as well. Test it by placing your head inside the container; if you see any light penetrating, it will not do. However, you can still use your container if you paint it, cover it or wrap it in bubble wrap for instance. Microorganisms and algae need very little light to start growing and this will cause you problems later on.

Submersible Pump

The majority of hydroponic systems make use of submersible pumps to get the nutrient solution to the chamber or root area from the reservoir where it is kept. Shops selling hydroponic systems will have these pumps in stock, in a variety of shapes and sizes. So will stores which sell garden supplies like fountains or water features.

A submersible pump uses electromagnets to make it spin the impeller. The pump should be cleaned regularly but it is very easy to dismantle them. Make sure your pump has a filter, otherwise add one using any sort of material similar to that used in furnace filter screens. This should also be cleaned regularly to function properly.

Delivery System

This is really only the method and equipment needed to get the nutrient solution to the root zone of your plants and then back to the reservoir. It consists of the submersible pump discussed in the previous paragraph and the connectors and tubing used to deliver the nutrient solution. The cheapest options are black or blue vinyl tubing, your standard irrigation tubing used for gardening or PVC connectors and tubing.

Maybe you want to add sprayers or drip emitters to your hydroponics system. That is fine but I would advise against it simply because they tend to clog and have to be cleaned out regularly. If you find them useful, make sure to keep extras which you can employ while you are cleaning the existing set. Remember that these will push up your costs.

Simple Timer

The need for a timer or two will depend on a few factors. If your hydroponic system does not receive natural light, you will need a timer which can control the timing for your artificial lights. Aeroponic systems, drip, and ebb and flow systems will also require timers for their submersible pumps. Certain kinds of aeroponics systems need special timers, so just be aware of that.

You do not have to buy specialized timers for your lighting or pumps; the standard light timers will work well. I recommend the so-called heavy duty or fifteen amps timers rather than those with only ten amps. It will state clearly on the package how strong it is. If you purchase the outdoor kind it should be water resistant and have a covering.

Many first-time hydroponic gardeners think they have to buy costly digital timers, but this is not necessary; the analogue type will work perfectly. Remember that a digital timer if it loses power or become unplugged accidentally for just a second will lose its settings and all memory. Usually the analogue types have just as many settings as the digital ones. Your timer should have pins around its dial all the way round.

Air Pump

Gardening systems which use water culture need air pumps but that is not always necessary with hydroponic systems. There are however, benefits to their use and they are really inexpensive, so you might as well buy one. Any store with aquarium supplies will sell them. An air pump makes sure your reservoir and plant roots receive enough oxygen and increases the air circulation. Air is pushed through the air tube and then through air stones, and in the process little air bubbles are created. These escape into the nutrient compound in the reservoir and float up.

If the plant roots are completely submerged in water all the time they will suffocate without enough oxygen. Therefore, water cultures need air pumps. Other kinds of hydroponics systems use air pumps in their reservoirs to increase the oxygen in the nutrient solution.

Air pumps have an added benefit; when these air bubbles in the water rise, they increase the circulation of the nutrients and water, distributing it more evenly. This circulation reduces the risk of pathogens establishing themselves in your reservoir easily.

Grow Lights

Plants will grow well in either artificial or natural sunlight. Sunlight will save you money and having to install extra equipment but the options are there. Grow lights will therefore only be necessary if the area you have available for your hydroponics system receives no sunlight. The seasons will also determine whether you need extra lights. Choose natural light if it is available to make it easier on yourself, but remember to check if the amount of sunlight your plants get is enough for them to flourish regardless of the season.

Do not try to use normal household lights; they are not the same as grow lights. The latter are especially designed to give off those wavelengths or color spectrums which mimic sunlight. These spectrums are necessary for photosynthesis. As we all know photosynthesis is essential for all plants to grow, produce flowers and fruit. It then follows that plants are affected greatly by the amounts of light they get in order to conduct photosynthesis.

In the next chapter I will discuss the common problems encountered for the various hydroponic systems. Read on so that you will be able to make an informed decision on which one will work best for your needs.

Chapter 3
Common Problems with Hydroponic Systems

It does not matter whether you purchased your system or constructed it yourself, you will encounter a few problems commonly experienced by gardeners. Amongst these are clogs, leaks, the inconvenience of using the system, the growth of algae, high maintenance (since they all seem to be temperamental to a certain extent), and lastly the expenses involved in re-using and maintaining various kinds of systems. In this chapter I will give you more information about these common problems and how to deal with them.

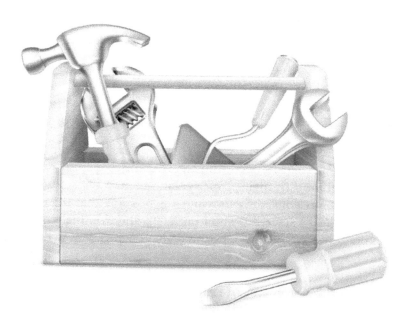

The Growth of Algae

A mixture of plant nutrients and water forms the bases of all hydroponics gardening systems and when you have these two elements combined with light, you are almost guaranteed to encounter algae growth. The problem is quite serious because fungus gnats are attracted by algae and they will cause damage to your plant roots. The best prevention is to limit the amount of light your nutrient solution gets, as much as possible. Use opaque or dark material to construct the reservoir and ensure it has a lid. The two tubes (the hose for the pump and the one for the water that returns to the reservoir) should fit snugly into their holes in the lids and not let in any light.

Your entire system should be as light proof as possible. One of the main weak spots of all systems is the holes made for the plants themselves. They should not be bigger than absolutely necessary to just hold your growth medium, for example a rockwool cube or netted pot. If you use a drip system which waters your growth medium from above, use a cap to cover the medium in order to lessen the areas that are exposed to light. Even drip emitters should be covered with light proofing. The only danger here is that you may fail to notice clogged emitters, so keep a watch out. All unused plant holes must be covered by an opaque or dark material.

Leaks in the Hydroponic System

A high pressure hydroponic system is more prone to leaks than a low pressure one. These leaks occur mostly when drip or spray emitters and stab fittings shift out of their proper positions. In a system where the nutrient solution is constantly flowing, it is possible that the root growth causes leaks since the water backs up and eventually spills out because the tubes are filled up. Fortunately, this problem is not such a common one.

Avoid most of the problems of leaks by installing a system which needs lower pressure. Examples of these are the NFT or DWC hydroponic systems. Another solution is to ensure your reservoir is big enough to accommodate the full quantity of nutrient solution which you use for the system and that your pipes and tubes are big enough to accommodate the water flow during all stages of root growth.

Clogging

Here is the main culprit; clogging causes more problems than anything else in spray and drip hydroponic systems. These systems usually make use of pumps with a high pressure to be able to force the nutrient compound through the tiny openings. Not even the implementation of filters and/or pre-filters will completely eliminate this problem, but it may reduce it. If this is your choice of system, prepare yourself to spend some time daily to check every single drip head and spray nozzle to ensure that they are still clog-free. You will have to keep a few extras to replace the clogged ones while you are cleaning them.

Convenience

Hydroponic systems need to be cleaned between each utilization and just how convenient it is to clean the entire system depends on a few factors. Access to each and every surface of your system is the answer. You need to be able to reach it with brushes and by hand. Holes which are really too small, unreachable bends and tight corners will only cause you headaches; you need to be able to reach every cranny with ease.

Secondly, with an easy to clean hydroponic system you should not have any problems to empty the reservoir without disturbing the roots of your plants too much. When you empty the system, try to get rid of all of the original solution. This changing process should be completed within 3 or 4 minutes. Always make sure your new nutrient solution is at room temperature before you replace the original one.

Temperamental Systems

Nobody likes to have to babysit and check their gardening system constantly throughout the day. All systems need daily attention; the nutrient solution for example, should be adjusted and checked once every day. However, some hydroponic systems need a lot more checking to avoid serious problems. Check your drip system twice or thrice during the day. Clogged emitters will leave your plant roots without their nutrient solution and even as little as two hours deprived of this nutrient solution could possibly kill them. This is especially the case if you use fast draining mediums.

Spray systems, principally an aeroponic system when interrupted, may likewise result in your plants being killed. Without the buffer of a growth medium to protect your plant roots, it will take less than one hour for them to die. So, if you fail to notice that your spray nozzle is clogged, it may cause serious problems.

Again, I recommend DWC or NFT systems, they are the least temperamental and most reliable. They require little maintenance and you only have to check them once every day, leaving you more time to do other things.

The Expense of Re-using and Cleaning Systems

If you re-use your hydroponic system, your main expense will be in replacing the growing medium of your plants. For example, for every new crop you will be obliged to get rid of all the rockwool you used previously, replacing it and this could be quite expensive, even if your system is a small one. Try using netted pots which are filled with lava rock or clay pellets for the growth medium; they are reusable and need not be replaced after every crop.

DWC and NFT systems need only a small quantity of growing medium. Mostly they grow the plants with their roots in a solution which is static and not moving and which has enough air bubbles to supply the oxygen the roots need. You will save a hefty sum of money in the long run if you do not have to replace the growth medium regularly and you will save yourself quite a bit of time and frustration on top of it.

In the next chapter I will discuss which plants are most successfully grown using a hydroponic system.

Chapter 4
Plants Best Suited for a Hydroponic Garden

It is a fact that not all plants are happiest in the soil free medium of aquatic gardening; some are more suited than others for a hydroponic system. I will now proceed to discuss the easiest fruit, herbs and vegetables to grow using this system. I will focus on those with the highest nutritional value. All of these can also be successfully grown aquaponically. This advanced hydroponics method combines aquaculture which is the raising of aquatic animals like fish, with the conventional hydroponic systems.

Spinach

We all know that spinach with its wonderful dark green leaves has many health benefits and should be part and parcel of any diet. In addition, it is one of the easiest veggies to grow in a hydroponic garden and will flourish in most hydroponic systems. You can harvest them as you need them, snipping off bits at a time or harvest your entire crop in one go. Spinach is a versatile vegetable and the tender young leaves can be served raw in a green salad or cooked in a variety of ways.

Lettuce

This crunchy salad ingredient is an old time favorite amongst both first time and experienced hydroponic systems gardeners. It grows easily and without fuss and you will be able to harvest those outer leaves continually while the rest of the plant continues growing. This will ensure a fresh green salad daily for you and your family. I recommend you start with Romaine, a healthy variety. The Bibb is also a popular choice.

Watercress

Watercress, like its name implies, just love water and will enjoy growing in your hydroponics garden. Because it does not last long after being cut, it is a very good choice if you want a fresh, crispy salad. Why settle for wilted watercress from the grocery store if you can have your own ready for the picking. It loves slightly alkaline water and if you use a system with moving water, it will thank you for it by flourishing.

Cherry Tomatoes

This beautiful fruit is not only an easy indoor grower; it is also well suited to hydroponic gardens. However, I should point out that all tomatoes, including the small cherry variety need lots of light, artificial or natural. To solve this problem, get an individual standing grow light just for your tomato plant or make use of a growing kit especially designed for cherry tomatoes, which comes with the LED lights your plant need.

Cucumbers

Just like tomatoes, cucumbers also need a decent amount of artificial or sunlight. This does not exclude them from your hydroponic garden though. This little hurdle can easily be overcome with a growing lamp and leave you with wonderful juicy cucumbers. Remember that the cucumber vines once they appear will need support in the form of a wire cage or large trellis. If your hydroponic garden is too small for support systems, choose the bush variety. Although their fruit is smaller in size, they are equally tasty and the seeds are readily available.

Peppers

I am sure you have seen plenty of indoor pepper plants in other gardeners' homes. The reason is that they look beautiful, and are easy growing, provided they receive ample light. Growth lamps are the solution if you consider them for your hydroponic system. However, if your hydroponics garden is inside your home and not inside a bigger green house, chili peppers might be a better choice. Seeing that your space is limited, these smaller varieties will flourish better than their larger bell pepper brothers and sisters.

Kale

In the last couple of years, you may have noticed the emerging popularity of this humble vegetable. That is because its health benefits are receiving more attention than previously. Unfortunately, kale is not often as available as other veggies and is often treated with pesticides when grown outside in soil. Kale grown in your own hydroponic garden will supply you with fresh produce without pesticides because bugs normally flying around in the open air cannot easily penetrate a hydroponics garden and a lot less pesticide is needed, if any.

Strawberries

Fresh strawberries are only found during the summer months, right? Wrong! Growing them in your own hydroponic garden system will make sure you have fresh fruit right through the year. And it is not difficult to grow them either. Plan ahead if you want to grow strawberries; after buying your strawberry runners, store them in your fridge for a couple of months, then install them in their proper place in your water based indoor garden. The cold temperature of the fridge jump starts them into growing so that you can expect them to flower very soon after you have planted them.

Mint

Most mint varieties are grown in soil, but water mint, also going by the name of orange mint, is an exception. It is semi aquatic and is usually found in the shallow water around streams and ponds. Peppermint, a cross between orange and spearmint, is also well suited to hydroponic gardens and love their watery environment. Even if you are not an experienced hydroponics gardener, you will be pleasantly surprised with your beautiful fragrant peppermint and orange mint plants.

Basil

Here is another fragrant herb to add to your list of plants for your hydroponic garden. Buy the seedlings from your local nursery, and then carefully get rid of all the soil by rinsing their roots under a small stream of water. Now they are ready to be transplanted and will reward you with fresh basil leaves for a long time.

Ready to start? Hang on a little bit before you run out to purchase everything you need, there is more information coming.

Chapter 5

Growing the Most Common Vegetables Hydroponically

In the previous chapter I discussed briefly which plants are fit and easy to grow in a hydroponic garden. In this chapter I will go into the nitty gritty of how exactly you should go about it. I will focus on a few vegetables in detail like peppers, tomatoes and salad greens which are well suited to this kind of gardening. I will also provide you with all the information on how to grow vegetables with small roots like green onions, beets and carrots, since they are just as happy to grow in a hydroponic system.

Lettuce (Lactuca Sativa)

Lettuce must be the most popular vegetable to grow using the hydroponic method and not only because it grows so quickly; you will be able to harvest your first lettuce leaves after barely a month. First the little lettuce seeds are germinated in a growth medium (without soil), and then they are transferred to the nutrient solution which will provide them with everything they need. You will need a relatively shallow container to hold the nutrient solution. On top of that you stack 4 polystyrene panels. These can be purchased at your local gardening center and is quite simple to construct. The panels have net pots to keep your lettuce plants in place. Florescent lights will provide ample light so that they can grow and mature right through the year, regardless of the season.

Germination of the Seedlings

1. Fill each plug tray with a soil-less growth medium. Now you have to moisten them, so add water slowly while you mix it well by hand. It should just be moist, not soggy. The seeds will rot if they are too wet.

2. Place 2 or 3 of the tiny lettuce seeds into each plug. Cover them with a quarter inch of the moistened growth medium. Now press down the growing medium carefully to make sure there is good contact between the seeds and their growth medium. Make sure you keep the medium moist right through the time of germination. The ideal temperature for the medium is between sixty and sixty-eight degrees Fahrenheit.

3. The minute you notice the little seedlings emerging, move them to any sunny location and provide them with florescent lights for around fourteen hours per day. The lights should be placed about two inches above your seedlings. Remember that lettuce prefers cool temperatures, so maintain the air temperature at below seventy-five degrees F. As soon as the plants reach two inches in height, thin them out, leaving only one strong seedling per plug.

The Hydroponic System(s)

1. Use a sharp kitchen knife to cut your 4 polystyrene panels to fit nicely over the nutrient solution container, stacking them neatly. Use one of the panels as a guide to make the marks where you will drill holes for your net pots. The holes should be twelve inches apart and the rows eight inches. Do not start right at the edge, but leave a space of four inches at the sides. For example, a panel of two by four feet will hold twenty-four net holes.

2. Use a saw drill with a two-inch bit to make the holes in the marked panel. Then continue with the other polystyrene panels, using the first one as your guide. The easiest way is to stack them carefully and then do your drilling. Lastly, place the net pots into their holes.

3. Now for your nutrient solution. Use clean water to fill the container you are going to use. There should be an air space measuring about one inch between the bottom of your panels and the top surface of the liquid. This will provide your plants with access to the oxygen they need. Now dissolve your ready mix nutrient solution into the clean water and place the panels with their pots on top of your container.

4. You are now ready to transfer the lettuce seedlings to their net pots. Do not pull them by their stalks; they can easily be killed this way. Rather slide your hand underneath them gently to remove them from their plug trays. A spoon also works well. Carefully loosen, and then straighten the plant roots before placing each seedling into its own net pot. Gently tuck at the little roots through the netting until they dangle in the nutrient solution underneath. I must point out again that your seedlings are only ready for their hydroponic home when they are about two inches tall. They will need to grow in their soil-less medium for two to three weeks first.

5. It is very important that your lettuce plants receive a minimum of fourteen hours light every day, so choose their location well, with enough sunlight and additional florescent lighting. Some evaporation will occur, so check the nutrient solution regularly and add water, maintaining the one-inch space above the solution. It is not necessary to add any additional nutrients solution, only water. Your lettuce plant should reach maturity within 5 to 6 weeks after germination. Any left-over nutrient compound solution after harvesting can be used for other house or garden plants.

What You Need

Here is a complete list of everything you need to assemble your hydroponic system:
- Net post, two inches
- Clean water
- Nutrient solution
- Drill bit, two inches
- Ruler and marker
- Shallow four to six-inch-deep plastic container
- Knife
- One-inch thick polystyrene panels
- Florescent lights
- Soilless growth medium
- Plug trays, three quarter inches.

Tips and Pointers

- Create home made net pots yourself. Take two-inch small sized plastic pots, cut half inch slats into their sides, leaving a rim two inches wide to keep their structure in place.
- Water mold like pythium or phytophthora can be avoided by cleaning out your trays with bleach after each crop. If you allow mold to develop, you will surely lose your entire crop.

- If you harvest your lettuces with their roots still attached, you will extend their storage life with two to four weeks.
- Instead of using a store bought growing solution, why not mix your own. Here is the recipe: Start with sixty-one gallons water. To this you add Chem-Gro (180 grams), magnesium sulphate (108 g), and calcium nitrate (180 g).
- Water which is too heavily chlorinated can sometimes affect lettuce plants adversely so try to make use of rain water, water from a well, or water which is lightly chlorinated.
- Do a regular inspection of your lettuce plants to check for any signs of powdery or downy mildew, or gray mold. Immediately remove infected plants.

Green Onions

Using only a few items of equipment, namely a number of four-inch pots, some polystyrene, soilless growth medium and a container which is waterproof, you can surprise your family by growing green onions either on small scale in your own kitchen window sill or more ambitiously on your patio or sun porch.

1. Choose the plastic container which will act as the reservoir for your hydroponic system. It can be one of the storage bins you already have in the house. Even a planter box lined with plastic will suffice. The main requirement is that it is completely water proof and it should be a minimum of six inches deep. Position your reservoir where it will receive between eight and ten hours sunlight every day.

2. Measure your reservoir and then proceed to cut a section of polystyrene (two inches thick) slightly smaller so that it fits inside the container and can float right on top of your nutrient solution. About a quarter to a one-inch difference should do the trick.

3. Draw a grid, six by six inches on this foam, using your yardstick and pencil. Now drill holes at every intersection with a hole saw with a three-and-a-half-inch bit.

4. Next, place plastic flowerpots (around four inches) into every hole in the foam. Use coconut coir, Rockwool or perlite as growth medium to fill every pot.

5. Put 4 little onion sets into each pot, spacing them out evenly. Then cover them with a one-inch layer of the planting medium you are using.

6. Prepare your nutrient solution by mixing hydroponic fertilizer and clean water. The instructions will be on the packet. The reservoir should be filled up to three inches from the top.

7. Carefully lower your foam float with the pots and plants onto the solution. You will have to add fertilizer, water or both to maintain your hydroponics system's liquid.

8. Check regularly for sneaky weeds or pests. They are usually not a problem but on and off some of these little problems might enter from the outdoors and attack your plants, especially if you grow them on your patio.

9. Your green onions will be ready for harvesting within 3 to 4 weeks. You can use the same pots immediately for your next crop.

What You Need

- Hydroponic fertilizer
- Clean water
- Measuring cups
- Onion sets
- Coconut coil, Rockwool or perlite
- Four-inch plastic flowerpots
- Electric drill, three and a half inches saw for drilling holes
- Yardstick and pencil
- Carving knife
- Polystyrene sheet, two inches thick
- A large container, waterproof.

Tips and Pointers

- You can grow green onions all year round in the US.
- Onion seeds can be started in dampened paper towels. When ready, use tweezers to pick them out and transplant gently in your pots with their planting medium.
- If you want a continuous supply of this vegetable, stagger your planting times.
- The hydroponics solution should be replaced every 4 to 6 weeks. Do not throw it out; use it for your vegetable garden or flowerbeds.

- As protection for your eyes, lungs and skin, don a dust mask as well as gloves when you mix the hydroponics solution and cut the polystyrene foam.
- Bear in mind that all water containers can be a drowning hazard for small children as well as pests, so take the necessary steps to keep everyone safe.

Onions

Onions grow easily in water; all they need is any sunny windowsill and a container with water. Within seven days their green sprouts will appear. These you can harvest continuously to use a in a number of different recipes and dishes.

1. Fill any glass jar to near the brim with water. In the water dissolve the required amount of fertilizer fit for onions as indicated on its box.

2. Choose the correct size onion to fit on top of your jar with its roots dangling in the water below. If your onion is too small, insert three toothpicks in to the bulb at the correct height so that only the roots will be in the water.
3. Do not move the toothpicks once you have inserted them; rather fill up with more liquid or remove some.
4. Choose any windowsill or a sunny area which will ensure your onions get sun for most of every day, or else make use of grow lights.

What You Need

- One of two grow lights
- Fertilizer
- Toothpicks
- A jar

Tips and Pointers

- Change the water/fertilizer solution weekly to prevent bacteria from growing.
- Be careful with the amount of fertilizer; too much can kill your onion.
- If no signs of life appear after about seven days, throw out the onion and replace with another one.

Potatoes

Gardening using the hydroponic method makes it possible for everyone, including city dwellers with only a small balcony or yard greenhouse to grow fruit or vegetables, and this includes potatoes. All you need is enough sunlight and the warm temperature inside your home to grow your veggies all year round. Of the many different hydroponic methods which exist, I would recommend the so-called aggregate method for potatoes. This method makes use of inert materials like perlite or pebbles as support for the plants and their root systems during its time of growth.

1. Buy seed potatoes at your local garden center. These will be either whole potatoes bulbs with a number of eyes or pieces of potatoes also with eyes. Your success rate will be better with seed potatoes as the store-bought ones are often treated specially to prevent them from sprouting and they may carry a number of diseases.

2. If you purchase whole potatoes, cut them into egg size pieces. Each piece should have a minimum of 2 eyes.

3. Place a plastic bin in a spot where it will receive six or more hours of sunlight daily. Use a half inch bit to make a line of drain holes along the upright sides. They should be 2 inches apart, as well as two inches above the bin bottom.

4. Fill your container up to two inches from the top with inert matter like perlite. If you are not familiar with this substance; it is broken up or crushed pieces of volcanic rock. It is light in weight and it has a moisture wicking character, making it the ideal medium for hydroponic gardening. Garden stores all stock perlite.

5. Pour enough water into your container until water starts to flow from the draining holes.

6. Now plant your seed potato pieces, around one inch deep into the perlite. If you use cut pieces, place them with their cut side facing down. Place a cover on your container. After around 2 weeks sprouts will start to appear. Keep the bin covered throughout, removing it only when you water your plants. They will need to be watered every 3 to 4 days.

7. As soon as the sprouts appear, add a liquid fertilizer weekly. The mixture is as follows: one-gallon water to one teaspoon 20-20-20 liquid fertilizer and add some micronutrients.

What You Need

- Liquid fertilizer
- Perlite
- A drill and half inch bit
- A plastic bin with a depth of ten inches or more
- Knife

Tips and Pointers

- When your plants have grown to a height of eighteen inches, start using a fertilizer with higher potassium content like 10-10-20. It will assist your potato tubers to mature.
- After seventy days you can expect to harvest your first potatoes.

Carrots

Carrots are equally simple and easy to grow hydroponically; you only need a few items and a little time. Here is how to go about it.

1. Use your drill to make 6 to 8 drainage holes all around a plastic bin (thirty-two quart). Drill them about three inches from the storage bin's bottom.

2. Select a sunny, warm location on a patio or deck or somewhere in your garden to put the bin.

3. Most carrot varieties suitable for containers are happy to grow in twelve-inch-deep perlite, so fill your bin to this depth or even deeper, depending on which specific variety you want to grow.

4. Moisten the top layer of the perlite slightly. Now place your carrot seeds onto the perlite, around half inches apart. Next you need to cover them completely with a half inch of perlite. Make sure to keep the seeds damp all the time. When they sprout and reach a height of two inches, you have to thin them out, keeping the strongest ones. They should now have a three-inch space around them.

5. As soon as your carrots have established themselves, fill up the bottom part of the plastic bin with a nutrient solution. All the extra solution will run out through the drainage holes, making sure that the nutrient solution does not get too deep. Just take care where you place your bin as you do not want this runoff to cause problems to other plants or your patio.

6. Keep the top layer of the perlite damp by sprinkling it lightly with the solution 2 or 3 times daily. Do not use too much, it really only needs to stay damp because your carrot plants will absorb most of their nutrient moisture from their reservoir underneath. Adjust the amount of solution you sprinkle them with according to the climate conditions. Keep this up until it is harvest time.

What You Need

- Watering can for sprinkling
- Fertilizer which can be dissolved in water, optional
- Epsom salt, optional
- Nutrient solution, hydroponic
- Perlite
- Quarter inch bit for drilling
- Drill
- Plastic bin, thirty-two quarts

Tips and Pointers

- If you lack space outside, place the carrots inside under grow lights. Put a tray underneath the bin to help with spills.
- Always follow the instructions on the label carefully if you make use of a concentrated nutrient solution. Here is a recipe for your home-made solution: For every gallon water, add two teaspoons micronutrient fertilizer (soluble), and one teaspoon Epsom salt.

- Carrot, as well as other root vegetables do not like too much moisture and will rot in too wet conditions, so choose a system which will not keep them soggy or in water constantly. If you keep their liquid level at three inches or less they will not stay wet constantly but still get enough water and food to grow to their full potential.

Beets

Root vegetables are best suited for beginner hydroponic gardeners. Caring for them is straight forward and hassle free and they grow fairly quickly. You will not wait too long before you can start harvesting and get your reward.

1. On average beets will grow to about one to two inches wide, therefore the containers you choose for them should have a diameter of at least four inches. They should also have a depth of at least six inches for those bigger roots.

2. If you grow them outdoors, choose an area which gets enough light; between 6 to 8 hours daily. Beets prefer temperatures of sixty to sixty-five degrees F. If you live in a cooler climate, set up your system in any enclosed space like a greenhouse where you can keep the temperature constant. Make sure your indoor area will also provide enough light, be it artificial or natural.

3. Fill the containers with either moss or sand to help to stabilize the beet seedlings. There should be a one-inch gap between your container top and the filler.

4. Now fill the watering container or tray of your hydroponic system with the fertilizer/water solution. Make sure to follow the instructions when you mix the water and fertilizer as different brands have different strengths. Usually the amount of fertilizer will be tiny compared to the water; around a teaspoon of the first to each gallon of the water. Mix extra solution and keep separately.

5. Mix these extra few cups you have kept with double the amount of water and keep in another shallow container. This will be used to soak your beet seedlings and give them some time to get used to the stronger fertilizer solution.

6. Before you put your seedlings into this container, rinse their roots to get rid of all the soil particles. Their adjustment period in the weaker solution need to be thirty minutes to one hour.

7. Remove your seedlings and transfer them to your hydroponic system. Remember that root vegetables like beet grow completely underground with just their leaves showing above ground, so make sure the beets are completely inside their containers, set firmly in the moss or sand. Each container should only house a single seedling.

8. You are now ready to start your hydroponic system so that the nutrient solution can flow to every plant. Check the level of the solution every day, adding more when necessary to maintain it at optimum level. In addition, check daily to make sure that the air zone between your container lids and the top level of the solution is maintained.

9. If the water level subsides, add more water, but don't add nutrients each time. It is only the water which evaporate, not the nutrients and adding more will make it too concentrated.

10. Only after ten to fifteen days should you fill your system with the same initial solution. Simply add this new solution to the container.

11. Keep on monitoring the water level, adding when necessary. Additional solution must be added again after a month. Beet seedlings in general will mature within forty to fifty days, so after forty days, start checking them often. As soon as your beets are one inch in diameter, they are ready to be harvested. Gardeners often let them grow to a diameter of two inches, so you may choose to grow your roots a bit bigger. However, any larger than that will result in less flavor.

What You Need

- Beet seedlings
- A shallow tray
- Measuring spoons and cups
- Hydroponics fertilizer for vegetables
- Moss or sand
- A hydroponics container system

Tips and Pointers

- Most garden stores sell hydroponic fertilizer. This is a nutrient compound especially designed for a hydroponic system. There are varieties designed for flowers, root vegetables, fruit or trees, so look out for the kind which is specifically mixed for root vegetables. In case a fertilizer bag does not provide a list of plants it is best suited for, find one which has a nutrient ratio of 5-10-10.
- Do not worry if in your eagerness you harvested your vegetables too early; young beets are already tasty and full of flavor.
- Do not throw out your beet leaves, they are edible too. They lend beautiful color and taste to a green salad and there are many other ways to incorporate them into your cooking.

In the next chapter I will tell you how to prepare your own home-made fertilizer. Many gardeners like to experiment with different mixtures from time to time to get the optimum growth from their plants. Once you have the basic recipes, you can start from there and as you become more experienced, maybe you can even improve on these.

Chapter 6

The Preparation and Use of Homemade Fertilizers

Just like in soil gardening, the plants you grow hydroponically are dependent on you to provide them with everything they need. In this instance their nutrients are in the hydroponic solution. One option is to purchase the ready-made concentrate from your hydroponic garden center and make up the nutrient solution by adding water. However, it is less costly and very easy to make up your own mixture at home. All you need are the basic ingredients.

Fertilizing Your Hydroponics

Plants grown in a hydroponics system do not come into contact with any soil, so they have to get everything necessary for their growth from the liquid solution you provide them with. That is why it is essential that this solution consists of all the required nutrients to fertilize them, or they will not be able to survive. This is what you have to do.

1. Start by pouring three gallons of clean water into a bucket.

2. Now add six teaspoons full of quality fertilizer to the water. The 20-20-20 mixture consists of 20% each of potassium, nitrogen and phosphorous. The mix should also have a complete range of trace elements and macronutrients. Trace elements are for example zinc, molybdenum and copper. Read the label to make sure all of these are found in the concentrated fertilizer you purchase.

3. The solution also needs magnesium sulphate and this can be found in Epsom salt. Three teaspoons will suffice.

4. Mix well until all the solids have completely dissolved into the water. Plants cannot absorb any solids, so make sure to break up all the lumps using a spoon or your hands so that the nutrients are dissolved in the solution.

5. Your fertilizer mix is now ready and you can pour it into the reservoir you are using.

What You Need

- A large spoon
- A bucket with capacity to hold four gallons. The bucket should have measures.
- Teaspoon
- Epsom salt
- Fertilizer (water soluble) containing macronutrients and trace elements

Tips and Pointers

- The variety of available fertilizers for hydroponic systems has a number of different formulations. Buy the one best suited for the specific plants you plan to grow if you are not yet ready to make up your own product. Simply prepare your mixture according to the instructions on the bag.

- Many hydroponic systems require pumps to bring about the movement and flow of the nutrient solution from the reservoir to the plants. Any solids in this solution will clog your system. To ensure your solution is lump-free, line a colander with layers of cheese cloth and pour your solution through it. Any lumps or little solid bits will be left in the colander. Systems which already contain filters will be less likely to clog but following the above recommendation might save you time and effort later on since filters are not always foolproof.

- Over time some evaporation will occur and the level of the nutrient solution will drop. Do not add more nutrients; just top up with clean water. Remember that the nutrients do not evaporate like water and if you add more, the solution may become too concentrated and this imbalance will cause harm to the plants. Only change the complete solution once every week or 2 so that it does not become too weak to feed your plants. Any signs like brown spots and/or yellow leaves tell you that your plants are experiencing problems and the first thing to do is to make up a fresh, new batch of nutrient solution immediately.

Making Liquid Fertilizer

Soil usually contains an abundance of minerals and micronutrients like iron and zinc, so commercial fertilizers do not normally contain these. The store-bought fertilizers focus on macronutrients like phosphorous, potassium and nitrogen. Because you are growing your plants hydroponically, no soil is present and you must provide all these essential elements needed by your plants by adding them to their liquid fertilizer.

Of course, you can buy specialized fertilizers, but they are expensive with the result that many hydroponic gardeners make their own liquid fertilizers. I would not recommend it if you plan to produce plants on a large scale, but for the home hydroponic gardener, they are reliable.

Worm or Compost Tea

1. Put one-pound worm castings or one-gallon compost in a five-gallon bucket.
2. Now fill up your bucket with clean water, mixing well.
3. Use an aquarium pump to aerate your mixture continuously.
4. Make sure your bucket is not in direct sunlight and leave it to sit for around 3 days. Stir each day.

5. Get rid of all the solid bits by straining this liquid through any filter. The remaining liquid can now be used to fertilize your plants.

Plant and Animal By-Products

1. Pour a gallon of clean water into a bucket or container.
2. Now add fish emulsion: one and a half teaspoons.
3. Next add seaweed extract: the same amount.
4. Lastly add blood meal: one tablespoon.
5. Stir the mixture well. If you need a larger volume, just use the exact same ratio.

What You Need

- Blood meal
- Seaweed extract
- Fish emulsion
- Measuring spoons
- Disposable filter
- Air pump, aquarium
- Five-gallon bucket
- Half a cup molasses
- Worm casings, one pound or compost, one gallon
- Clean water

Tips and Pointers

- The following is a list of the essential elements plants need for growing: Chlorine (Cl), molybdenum (Mo), zinc (Zn), copper (Cu), manganese (Mn), boron (B), magnesium (Mg), iron (Fe), calcium (Ca), sulphur (S), nitrogen (N), potassium (K), phosphorus (P), oxygen (O), hydrogen (H), and carbon (C).
- It is a complicated process to formulate liquid fertilizers directly using mineral salts and nutrients. It might actually only be worthwhile if you already have a twenty-gallon container and plan to use a large hydroponic system for your gardening.

Making Hydroponic Nutrient Solutions

It is possible to make your own nutrient mixture suitable for a hydroponics garden and it will not empty your purse either.

1. Pour clean water into either a tank, tub or bucket with the same capacity as your hydroponic reservoir. Measure how many gallons you add.

2. If you do not already have one, purchaser a pH test kit especially designed for hydroponic systems from your hydroponic supplier. It should also contain an adjustment kit. Now measure the pH level of your water in the container. The reading should lie between five and six. If it does not lie in this range, adjust it using the chemicals provided until the desired pH level is achieved.

3. Add two teaspoons dry fertilizer for every gallon water. The fertilizer must be dissolvable. Your fertilizer should contain the complete range of macronutrients like sulphur, nitrogen, calcium, magnesium, phosphorus, and potassium. On top of this, the fertilizer must also have the necessary micronutrients like cobalt, iron, chlorine, copper, manganese, boron, molybdenum and zinc.

4. Next add a teaspoon Epsom salt for every gallon of clean water.

5. Stir well until no more crystals or powders are visible and everything has dissolved.

6. This nutrient solution should be removed and replaced every 1 or 2 weeks so that all your plants have a continuous supply of their essential nutrients.

What You Need

- A stick or large spoon
- Epsom salt

- Fertilizer, both water soluble and containing macro and micro nutrients
- A teaspoon
- A pH test kit with adjustment chemicals
- A gallon jug/ measuring cup
- Container such as a bucket or tub.

Tips and Pointers

- Before you start mixing, make sure what the capacity of your reservoir is so that you make up the required amount of nutrient solution.
- Also use a big enough container so that you do not have spills when you stir and mix the solution.
- Make up your solution shortly before you plan to use it. If you store it, some of its strength may be lost over time.
- Some evaporation will occur so when you see the level drop because of that or absorption, add only clean water. You do not want to create an imbalance or salt build-up by adding more nutrients.
- Use this home-made fertilizer if you have an ebb and flow or raft system which is not likely to clog. Hydroponic environments like an aeroponic system or a drip method might clog up the nozzles if particles of solids are present.

Growing Hydroponically Without Chemicals

The essential elements plants need to grow can be either from organic or man-made sources. Maybe you prefer the organic option and want to stay clear of a hydroponics soup filled with all kinds of chemicals. I have to warn you; going the natural way might be more difficult; you will not know exactly what your plants are absorbing from their water, but on the other hand, your crop will be hundred percent organic.

Home-Made Organic Tea

1. Use either worm casings, compost or both to fill any large container halfway full. The compost or casings should be brown and have a dirt-like, crumbly look; then you know it is really well-aged.

2. Now fill up nearly to the container's top with clean water. Mix everything well and allow to stand for a minimum of one day. By this time the water will have turned brown.

3. Strain the liquid through a few layers of cheese cloth placed inside a colander.

4. This is the liquid you will be using in your reservoir, so there are no man-made fertilizers involved.

5. Check your plants daily for any signs of deficiencies as far as their nutrient intake is concerned. If you notice anything untoward, replace their nutrient solution one or two times every week; even more frequently if necessary.

Commercial Organic Products

1. Pour clean water according to the amount you need into the reservoir of your hydroponic system or into any other container.

2. Measure out two teaspoons of the commercially produced organic fertilizer to every gallon of clean water and then add to the water.

3. Also add a teaspoon Epsom salt to the same amount of water. Epsom salts is a natural product of nature.

4. Mix well by stirring until everything has dissolved. This liquid should be replaced once every week.

What You Need

- Epsom salt
- Organic fertilizer (commercial)
- A measuring spoon
- Cheese cloth
- Colander
- Worm casings and/or compost
- Two large buckets

Tips and Pointers

- Organic nutrients for hydroponic gardens are available but tend to cost more. If you are pressed for time and do not want to go to the expense or all the effort of making your own, you may choose to simply buy this product.
- Hydroponic systems that use pumps can easily clog and cause many problems. Make sure no little particles of matter are left in your organic tea by straining it more than once.
- It is difficult to determine the nutrient level of organic solutions. Therefore, you have to pay special attention to your plants and check them regularly for any distress signs like brown spots, odd colors or yellow leaves. This may be an indication that they are not receiving sufficient nutrients. Immediately replace the organic tea in your reservoir.

After reading this chapter you may still have a few questions or uncertainties. Do not worry; in the next section I will answer all of the frequently asked questions and you will have all the answers you need.

Chapter 7
Frequently Asked Questions

How Long Must I Keep My Grow Lights On?

While plants are vegetating, they need around eighteen hours of proper light per day. As soon as they start to flower, or has grown enough to start the flowering process, the hours may be reduced to twelve hours of light followed by twelve hours of darkness. Please keep in mind; plants which are flowering need uninterrupted darkness for twelve hours. If they receive light during this period they may return to the vegetative state or even mutate which is worse because it will have a massive impact on the final result.

Why are my plants dying?

There are many different reasons why plants die. I suggest you start with the most obvious reasons like broken stems, not enough or no water at all, or too high temperatures.

Once you have eliminated these causes, you will have to investigate further. So-called sudden deaths of plants are mainly due to root diseases. These diseases may result in plants not yielding or even the death of your plants. Amongst root diseases Pythium or root rot is most commonly encountered and is usually the result of poor drainage and over irrigation.

Temperature control is also very important and could cause endless problems if not adhered to. If you struggle to maintain the correct temperatures in your reservoir, make use of nutrient conditioners. These formulations contain quaternary copper and ammonium that help to prevent those nasty pathogens developing.

Why are the Tips of My Plant Leaves Burned?

In general, this is a sign that your plants are receiving too much salt. Adding too much nutrients can lead to an imbalance and build-up of salt in the reservoir. Do not add nutrients every time when the water level drops; only clean water. Flushing your reservoir regularly will help to prevent this problem.

I suggest you use Cyco pharmaceutical nutrients. They can be used for any consumable crops and are perfectly safe.

Other nutrient deficiencies may also result in burned tips of plant leaves. Make sure the nutrient solution you use is fit for your specific plants.

Why are the Leaves of my Plants Turning Yellow?

This is a more difficult question to answer as there can be a number of reasons why leaves start turning yellow. They all prevent your plants from absorbing the correct quantities of nutrients. I recommend you go through the list of factors and check them one by one.

- The oxygen levels are too low. This may be the result of over-irrigation or the lack of adequate aeration.
- Nutrient deficiencies.
- There might be a build-up of salt in your reservoir.
- The temperature of your nutrient solution may either be too high or too low.
- The pH level of the water in your reservoir may be incorrect.

Why are my Plants Stretching?

There are two main reasons why plants stretch. The first is because they do not receive adequate light. Either your grow lights are placed too far from the plants or you do not provide them with enough light and they have to compete for the available light and start to stretch toward the light source. Secondly, the humidity in your hydroponic garden is too high. If the temperature of your nutrient solution is too high is may lead to bolting and you will lose your crop.

What is the Correct Humidity?

Keep the humidity at between forty and seventy percent during the vegetative and growing periods. While your plants are flowering or blooming it should be lowered to between forty and fifty five percent. For curing and storing strive for between fifty and sixty three percent humidity.

As I have mentioned before, the correct humidity level is of the utmost importance. Grey mould will develop very quickly in long periods of excessive humidity and once it has started, it will spread rapidly to infect your whole crop.

Install a hygrometer where it is easily visible inside your green room or hydroponic area. Check it every time you enter this room and more frequently if you start to detect fluctuations. An average humidity of under fifty percent is good; do not allow it to rise higher than that. An easy way to control the humidity is to cover your reservoirs as they may contribute to a raise in the humidity.

Installing extractor and inlet fans will greatly assist in keeping the correct temperature and humidity levels. Always try to keep the hydroponic rooms dry; mould is less likely to develop in dry conditions.

Is Ventilation Necessary and How Much Should I Provide?

The simple answer is yes; your plants do need good ventilation. Ventilation keeps the temperature and humidity in check. Measured in the middle section of your hydroponic plant canopy, the temperature should be around sixty-eight degrees F and the humidity around fifty-five to sixty percent. The inside temperature should correspond to that outside except in winter when it should correspond to the ambient humidity and temperatures.

Do I Have to Prune My Plant Leaves?

No. Because the plants need such a long period of time to grow their leaves it can be harmful to some of them if you remove any of the larger leaves. It will set back their development.

Do I have to Aerate my Nutrient Solution?

It is always a very good idea to, yes. Not only does it keep the water moving around and keep it from stagnating, it will prevent all kinds of bacterial infections. You will extend the health period of the nutrient solution if you aerate it as well, so that it can last much longer than a solution which is just sitting there.

Does it Take Long for Plant Clones to Develop Roots?

It will depend on whether the specific method used for cloning was assisted or manual. Most manually cloned plants will take around five to twelve days. Assisted cloning makes use of machines which speed up the oxygen intake of the plants drastically, resulting in the development of roots within three to seven days.

The time needed to strike roots also varies according to the overall health of these clones and of course the season.

What Kind of Water Should I Use?

The cleaner the water, the better. And by clean water I mean water that is free of contaminants and low in salt. I recommend rain water, but if that is not available, water from the tap will be quite satisfactory. More and more gardeners make use of water that has been cleaned by reversed osmosis. There is a downside however; pH fluctuations may occur and need to be corrected with a stabilizer. This kind of water also needs to be reconditioned with magnesium calcium additives afterwards.

As a Beginner, How Do I Set Up my Grow Room?

Any room can potentially be converted into a hydroponics grow room – a shed, your garage or a store room. However, there are a few considerations you should pay attention to when deciding on which area to select.

We all know that in outdoor gardens plants grow best in a warm sunny spot. These conditions are perfect for most plants. The plants in your hydroponic room need exactly these same conditions, so this is what you have to strive to create for them. The three main aspects you have to focus especially on are light, humidity and light.

Should I Use Grow Lights in my Grow Room?

Lighting is the one element your plants cannot live without. No hydroponic room should be without proper lighting. An outdoor greenroom will need less artificial lighting but if your grow room is located in your cellar or any area which has normal roofing, it is important that you create the same light conditions you would encounter in that sunny spot in the garden.

Fortunately, with the horticultural technology that exists today, you can purchase grow lights which mimic sunlight and are cost effective and efficient. For any indoor hydroponic gardening I recommend that you use grow lighting exclusively without depending on light form skylights or windows. Grow lights can easily be controlled and set to switch on or off as required.

With artificial lighting you can grow your plants regardless of the time of year. Long summer days can be recreated inside your grow room by extending the hours of light you give your plants. This will assist them during their growth spurt. You can simulate autumn with less hours of lighting to encourage your plants to commence their flowering. A well designed and controlled grow room will produce wonderful results and open up possibilities to grow almost any variety of plant.

HID Lighting: What is It?

HID stands for lights with a high intensity discharge. They are number one amongst grow lights and I strongly recommend that you purchase these. In hydroponic gardening three different types of these grow lights are available: MH or Metal Halide, HPS High Pressure Sodium, and CMH or Ceramic Metal Halite.

Are These Lights Safe to Use Inside My Home?

These growing lights are all quite safe to use. They are used everywhere; in street lights, gas stations, grocery stores, and retail. Even the security lights in most backyards are HID lights. Lighting fixtures and systems which are safe are all UL tested.

Why are HID Lights Good for my Hydroponic Plants?

They are good because they provide a very intense source of lighting for your indoor plants. They are efficient and cost effective since they will last more than 6 times as long as the other types of grow lights.

Could I Use Florescent Lights?

Use florescent grow lights for your seedlings and clones. You may also make use of them for supplementary lighting but rather use HID grow lights for your hydroponic grow room.

Well, I am sure I have now answered all those nagging questions you had. It is now time to start on your hydroponics endeavor.

Conclusion

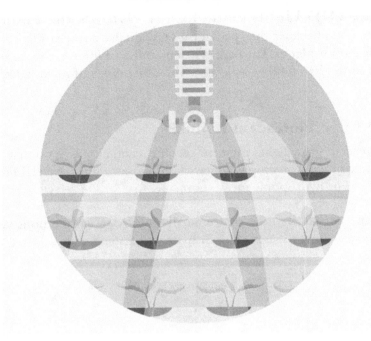

If you have read this far, I can conclude that you are really serious about starting your own hydroponic garden at home. Well done! You have taken the first and most important step; getting all the information you need. Now you can go ahead and make a list of the plants you want to start growing. Then make another little list of the few basics you need to purchase or assemble at home and you are ready.

I also want to congratulate you on making the right choice. The benefits of using hydroponics are many-fold. You are now making your contribution to keeping the environment healthy. In the first instance the use of pesticides which is part and parcel of most traditional gardening methods, is eliminated. Because you grow your plants in a controlled space, you should not have any problems with pests. Your vegetables can be grown completely organically, so you are putting yours and your family's health first.

Secondly, a lot less resources are needed to grow your vegetables if you use hydroponic methods. The water used for the nutrient solution is recycled and re-used, which means that you use less. No spill-offs will occur which can damage the environment like in traditional gardening.

Lastly hydroponic gardening is a lot less labor intensive. You are working in a compact space and can arrange all your plants at waist-high level so that you do not need to go down on your knees or bend down all the time. You will also save lots of time.

With all these benefits in mind I am sure you need no more convincing. So, go out and make a start. In no time you will be able to harvest your first crops and enjoy your wonderful healthy home-grown vegetables, filled with flavor and goodness. Not only will you impress your friends with your organic produce but you may just convince them to start their own hydroponic gardens as well; especially if they see how easy, mess-free and space-saving it really is.

Other Related Books

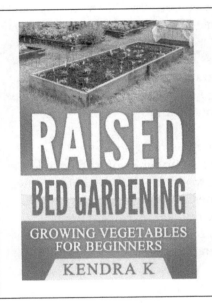

Raised Bed Gardening: Growing Vegetables for Beginners

ISBN-13: 978-1546439943
ASIN: B0727Y5S1T

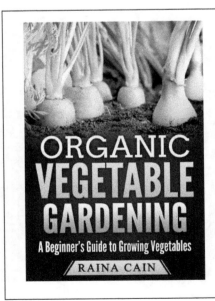

Organic Vegetable Gardening: A Beginner's Guide to Growing Vegetables

ISBN-13: 978-1985040878
ASIN: B079KHC3XB

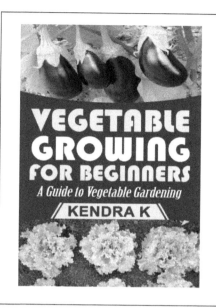

Vegetable Growing for Beginners: A Guide to Vegetable Gardening

ISBN-13: 978-1545415115
ASIN: B071XSV5BS

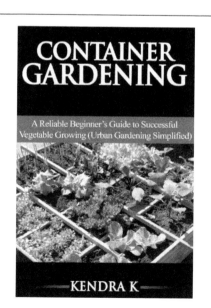

Container Gardening: A Reliable Beginner's Guide to Successful Vegetable Growing (Urban Gardening Simplified)

ISBN-13: 978-1517773762
ASIN: B014AO0JMK

Indoor Herb Gardening: A Beginner's Guide to Growing Herbs

ISBN-13: 978-1976264306
ASIN: B075JFTF8V

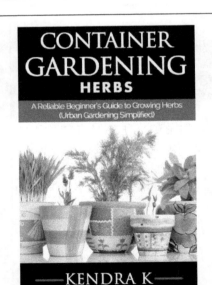

Container Gardening: A Reliable Beginner's Guide to Growing Herbs (Urban Gardening Simplified)

ISBN-13: 978-1517646363
ASIN: B015G6ZVO2

Tomato Growing: A Beginners Guide to Plump & Juicy Tomatoes

ISBN-13: 978-1545073933
ASIN: B06Y2K6BQT

www.ingramcontent.com/pod-product-compliance
Lightning Source LLC
LaVergne TN
LVHW021734301224
800254LV00010B/788